# Queen Elizabeth II:
# A Lasting Tribute

Christian WJ Catsanos

BookLeaf
Publishing

Presentation by *BookLeaf Publishing*

Web: www.bookleafpub.com

E-mail: info@bookleafpub.com

ISBN: 978-93-95784-44-3

First edition 2022

# DEDICATION

To the memory of Queen Elizabeth II, and to
King Charles III

# Farewell

Farewell, my lovely Queen;
None brighter e'er than thee I knew,
None e'er so great, the whole world through
My eyes did see.

Farewell, Elizabeth;
Thy body rests in earthly night,
But doth thy spirit into light
Follow by death.

Thy people look to thee,
And pray to God in heav'n above,
That thou be seated in His love
Eternally.

# The beauteous Queen

The beauteous Queen of our dear motherland,
Who sev'n great decades sat upon her throne,
With loving care within her pow'rful hand,
From this her earthly dwelling-place is gone.

Her people always held within her mind,
Ne'er did she to her selfish whims take heart;
Forever was she dutiful and kind,
Her gifts unto her people to impart.

And yet, her time is up, God rest her soul,
That lives forever in the heav'nly height,
Where all that once was broken is made whole,
And all the depths of darkness turn to light.

As in her life, we love her in her death,
Our Sov'reign Lady Queen, Elizabeth.

# Elizabeth

Elizabeth
The Queen of our dear land

Elizabeth
Such love was in thy hand

Elizabeth
Long was thy glorious reign

Elizabeth
Now heav'n dost thou attain

Elizabeth
Take now thine endless rest

Elizabeth
In God may thou be blest

# Thou unexpected Queen

(This is envisaged to be sung to the tune
composed by Michael Head for the text "The
little road to Bethlehem")

When thou wert born, to thee was it not known
That thou would sit upon Great Britain's throne.
Young Edward still was King to be, by right;
But as it was, new happ'nings came to light.

Young Edward placed the crown in disarray,
Until did come his abdication day;
And then Prince Albert did become King
George,
The pathway of thy future life to forge.

For thus the greatest reign was brought to birth,
And thy sev'n decades marvelled all the earth;
And so to think it almost ne'er had been
Thy place in life, Thou unexpected Queen.

# Beautiful lady

5

(This is envisaged to be sung to the tune composed
by the Sisters of Notre Dame around 1910 for the text
"Guardian Angel, from heaven so bright")

Beautiful lady, the light of my land;
Ne'er did one fair as thee in thy place stand!
All England's glory was in thy fair face,
For thou didst never thy duties erase!

Beauteous Elizabeth, in thy sweet rest,
England thy glory shall ever be blest.

Queen of my country, and heart of my love,
Ne'er from thy beautiful face could I move;
All of my life I no other have known,
Thou and thou only didst sit on the throne.

Beauteous Elizabeth, in thy sweet rest,
England thy glory shall ever be blest.

Though thou art sadly amongst us no more,
England shall blossom as ever before;
For all thy kinfolk, each dutiful heir,
Heed thine example, that thou wert still there.

Beauteous Elizabeth, in thy sweet rest,
England thy glory shall ever be blest.

# Philip thy Love

(This is envisaged to be sung to the tune DIX
composed by Conrad Kocher)

Love is patient, love is kind;
O what love thy heart did find!
Thou wert young, when Philip came
To thy heart, ne'er more the same!
For he was thy love and life,
He thy husband, thou his wife.

Those threescore and thirteen years
Banished sorrows, banished tears.
For whate'er did come thy way,
By thy side would Philip stay:
He would be thy strength and guide;
Thou the glory of his side.

Reunited with thy love,
Philip sweet, in heav'n above,
Thou shalt rest in perfect peace,
With a love that ne'er shall cease;
And, as endless days shall be,
Philip shall be love to thee.

# Dutiful servant Queen

(to be sung to the traditional "God save the Queen [King]" melody)

Dutiful servant Queen,
A handmaid thou hast been
To God above.
King of all heav'n and earth,
Who brought thy throne to birth;
All thine intrinsic worth
Is in His love.

He is the mighty God,
Thou in His stead hath trod
Upon the throne.
Knowing thy lowliness,
His might didst thou confess;
Thus did He richly bless
All thou hast known.

Servant of God above,
Knowing a heav'nly love,
In Him now rest.
Near His eternal throne,
A place dost now thou own,
More than was ever known,
Where thou art blest.

# O gentle, humble Queen

(This is envisaged to be sung to the tune ST
THOMAS composed by Aaron Williams)

O gentle, humble Queen
Who served thy people long;
None e'er so great as thee was seen,
None e'er so bold and strong.

Who didst thy people love,
And always bear in mind;
With faithful service e'er to prove
That thou to them wert kind.

Now take thy hallow'd rest,
Now that thy reign is done;
And join the glory of the blest
In God, whom rest hath won.

# Elizabeth my love

(This is envisaged to be sung to the tune ST
THOMAS composed by Aaron Williams)

Elizabeth my love,
The Sov'reign of my heart,
Who didst thy people's spirits move,
Amazing that thou art!

The love of all thy land,
Who held thee in their love;
Take now thy place near God's own hand
In heav'n's great realm above.

Thy people love thee still,
And long as they shall live,
To God, for thee, thy people will
Their supplications give.

# Thy jubilees

Thy silver jubilee,
That quarter cent'ry on the throne,
E'en then was all thy goodness known.

Thy golden jubilee,
Though were thy moth'r and sister gone,
Thou after fifty years liv'dst on.

Thy diamond jubilee,
Frail Philip was not by thy side,
In sickness still with thee to'abide.

Thy platinum jubilee,
Though old and frail, with Philip gone,
The world stood firm and loved thy throne.

# Princess Elizabeth's war-torn childhood

Princess Elizabeth,
In childhood didst thou know of war,
Divided lands as ne'er before,
And wasteful, senseless death.

Though war was fraught with woe
To England did thy father cleave,
Proclaiming he would never leave,
Thou nowhere else didst go.

These scars, for all thy life,
Wouldst still thou bear, knowing that war
Could tear a land like ne'er before,
In pangs of deadly strife.

# Forever in our hearts, dear Queen

(This is envisaged to be sung to the tune
TALLIS' CANON composed by Thomas Tallis)

Forever in our hearts, dear Queen,
Who o'er thy people loved to reign;
Though thou art gone from earthly sight,
We see thee in our Saviour's light.

For all the good that thou hast done,
The Lord's great friendship hast thou won,
Where sit the saints in all their grace,
Beholding their sweet Saviour's face.

Forevermore shalt now thou stay
In God's own house, where thou for aye
Shalt sing the songs of those who love
The Saviour God in heav'n above.

# We love thee, Queen Elizabeth

We love thee, Queen Elizabeth,
Just as in life, so still in death,
To know thy beatific breath.

Thou art with God, deep in his love,
Where ne'er our sins and failings move,
In His great heav'nly home above.

Still in our hearts forevermore,
We love thee now, just as before;
And with thee, we our God adore.

# My Queen and my Lady

(This is envisaged to be sung to the tune THE
ASH GROVE)

My Queen and my Lady, the love of my nation,
The glory of England, the joy of my heart.
I love thee sincerely for all thou hast giv'n us;
My Sov'reign and Lady forever thou art.
Though now thou art with us no more in this
nation,
But dwelling with God in His Kingdom above,
I still, in my own heart, hold thee in my keeping,
The Queen of my nation and Lady of love.

# My dearly lovèd Queen

(This is envisaged to be sung to the tune
REDFIELD composed in 2015 by Christian WJ
Catsanos for the hymn text "Why do I sigh to
find" by Henry Francis Lyte)

My dearly lovèd Queen,
My heart shall miss thee each and ev'ry day;
And yet I know that thou didst tread God's way,
And sharest now His reign.

Thy place in heav'n's great height,
Where God doth reign with all his saints above,
From which thou dost thy subjects always love,
Is now thy heart's delight.

Elizabeth my love,
Remember me before thy Father's throne,
Remember too, all subjects thou didst own,
Unto their God above.

# My heart now aches for thee

(This is envisaged to be sung to the tune GOPSAL
composed by Georg Friedrich Händel)

My heart now aches for thee,
Elizabeth my Queen,
Who is now gone from me,
By God in heav'n now seen!

Elizabeth, thy heart of love
Now dwelleth with thy God above!

Didst thou heed God's command
With faithful heart and soul;
And gavest thy great hand
Unto thy folk, in whole!

Elizabeth, thy heart of love
Now dwelleth with thy God above!

Be evermore my Queen,
Though dwellest thou above;
That all my needs be seen
By our great God of love!

Elizabeth, thy heart of love
Now dwelleth with thy God above!

# Queen of Australia, too

Though England was thy happy home,
Thou wert the glorious Queen
Of many other lands beside,
Where too thy love was seen.

Though England in thy heart was dear,
The service of thy love
Was giv'n to all across the globe
Who in thy realms didst move.

Queen of all England, and the realm,
Still all thy people knew
That thou wert truly, truly so:
Queen of Australia, too.

# God save good Charles, our King

(to be sung to the traditional "God save the King" melody)

God save good Charles, our King!
Now may his people sing,
Both near and far.
Be his reign great and long,
And be his sceptre strong,
And be his joyful song:
Alleluia!

May all his people see
True life and liberty,
Where'er he reign:
Grant him abundant wealth,
And mind's and body's health,
And all the Commonwealth
For his domain!

Hear Thou the song, now sung
By ev'ry creed and tongue,
We to Thee bring:
"May we Thy name adore,
And may we Thee implore,
Both now and evermore:
God save the King!"

CPSIA information can be obtained
at www.ICGtesting.com
Printed in the USA
BVHW052309030723
666720BV00007B/239